Using Your Intuition By Psychic Tony Hindley

The Contents

With thanks - Tony's thanks

The Reason - Why the book has been written

In the Beginning

The Development Begins

Spiritual Protection

Spirit Energies I work with

Meditation - Purpose of Meditation

Working alongside Spirit Guides - Spirit Guides

Meditation / Healing room

Development

Higher Self

Conclusion

Connect with Tony

Supernatural Diaries Team & Photos

References

Using Your Intuition By Psychic Medium Tony Hindley

With Thanks

Firstly I would like to thank you for buying this book, Thank you for choosing this book to help you in your development in your spiritual direction and path. I would also like to take this time to dedicate this book to a few people within my life who have taken the transition into the spirit world.

My Great Grandmother Mary Hindley

20/05/1900 - 20/03/-1996

My Uncle Brian Hupton

13/02/1972 - 17/09/2014

My Grandmother Joan Hindley

27/04/1929 - 02/01/2017

My Grandfather Brian Hupton

10/06/1941 - 03/02/2018

My Uncle Henry Gleave

04/12/1926 - 12/03/2018

Using Your Intuition By Psychic Medium Tony Hindley

With Thanks

These people have given me the courage and passion within my direction, all believing in me and trusting my path. Never judging and never ignorant, only ever interested in my belief, even if their belief was and still is different.

My family I thank you for allowing me to be me, trusting in me and telling me all will be ok, even when I felt I had failed you pushed me and trusted me and that is worth more than you understand. Each one of you keep me grounded and safe.

My friends and the people who have followed my work, Thank you to each and every one of you for believing in my work, giving me the sense of purpose within my life and direction. Through the hard times within my life you have stood by me and believed in me, always giving me the push and kick to continue and to never give up.

Using Your Intuition By Psychic Medium Tony Hindley

With Thanks

My Team who work alongside me. Ryan following my work from the very start, supporting me and pushing me. Dawn your trust in my work from day one, Alison your words of advice and support, Michelle your belief in me. Everyone of you are amazing in your own right. You truly are fantastic friends.

My partner Kevin, assisting me from day one, picking me up and telling me I am worth more than I can imagine, bringing back my confidence that had been taken away from me. You truly are a force to be reckoned with.

Dreams and goals can come true, all you need to do is believe in yourself and have loving support from positive people within your life. Don't place barriers overcome them.

"Everything you can imagine is real" - *Quoted by Albert Einstein*

Using Your Intuition By Psychic Medium Tony Hindley

The Reason

At first when people asked me to write this book, I became rather confused and asked myself why? I'm just Antony, not some famous person who is within the public eye, I'm just little old me.

A lot of people believe in my work and some people don't. I am not here to preach or tell people what is right and what is wrong. I believe within my mind, body and soul, that I have been given this ability to share, whether people believe or not. I am a great believer in respecting others and others beliefs. I truly hand on my heart believe this is why my ability has grown in such a rapid way. This book is all about intuition and using this to your highest ability. There are many books out there, TELLING you how to read cards, connect to the spirit world, read auras (To name just a few) and gives you the authors interpretation. So when you decide to do a sitting, one to one,

Using Your Intuition By Psychic Medium Tony Hindley

The Reason

Session (you may refer to your readings differently) you're actually not giving your interpretation, you are giving the authors. This book will explain to you and give you examples of how I work as a Psychic Medium. It will allow you to understand what I mean by the term "Using Your Own Intuition".

Working alongside spirit has opened my eyes and mind to many possibilities. Understanding yourself inside and out is the main thing I have understood as a human being / spirit energy. This has allowed me to find deep within, my own ways to develop and increase my personal connection to the spirit world. Do not be cloned into someone else. We are all individual and we all have many unique gifts. We are all in our own paths, sharing and trying to understand this together. I say trying as we can never understand the spirit world fully and how our gifts have been given or passed down to us. I

Using Your Intuition By Psychic Medium Tony Hindley

The Reason

Am not your teacher, your guide or your tutor. I am Antony, a young man who has been given an opportunity by the spirits to lighten your spiritual way. Assisting you to find, your inner confidence and your inner self. People often ask how do I connect, I connect with Honesty, Truth, Direction, Loyalty to spirit and those around me and most of all to me TRUST! When reading I consider myself as the "vessel". Allowing and trusting my guides to connect me with the other side. Having Truth, Honesty, Direction and Loyalty within your life path, will allow the natural connection to the spirit world, but it will also give you that inner confidence and belief that you are TRUE!

Believing in yourself, having the inner confidence to not fear failure, accepting the positive around you and dismissing the negative feelings. Has given me the connection that I hold today.

Using Your Intuition By Psychic Medium Tony Hindley

In the Beginning

I grew up in a little town called Atherton, not too far from the city of Manchester. I was raised in a working class family, with my Mum (Susan), Dad (Peter) and my older (but not taller) brother John. Growing up I knew I was different from other people, little did I know how different I was actually going to become. I am the first person within my blood line to hold this "Unique Gift". I say unique simply because it is a Blessing to have the ability to communicate with the spirit world. This isn't my job, this is my life

My connection to the spirit world started at the young tender age of six. I remember it like it was yesterday.

At the time we had two very large dogs, Mindy & Sadie. I was sitting in my bedroom with the dogs sitting beside my bed. In fact I should have been going to sleep, but I was too busy chatting to a small lady with a big belly. She said to me

Using Your Intuition By Psychic Medium Tony Hindley

In the Beginning

"Hi Antony, I am your grandmother Lilly". She visited me several times during my younger days and It was years later when I found out who she was. This lady was certainly my grandmother, she was my grandmothers mother from my mother's side of the family, a cheeky character and certainly not shy. I remember being in school and seeing her there watching me and keeping me safe. I would talk to her on a regular basis. This happened for many of years and continued into my teenage years. Then all of a sudden when I needed her the most she wasn't there, now I know why.

I started high school and to say the first few years where hard is an understatement. I had a brilliant school life during the day, but as soon as the bell rang I would get my things and run all the way home. This was due to the bullies waiting for me and I wanted to get home quickly. A few times they did catch up with me

Using Your Intuition By Psychic Medium Tony Hindley

In the Beginning

And would call me and hit me. Upset and scared from this as a child I didn't understand why people where so unkind. I continued my life at school feeling a little lost as to why this lady I had spoken to for many years had suddenly vanished. The bullies continued for while and then one evening I was invited to the local "Fair ground". I met friends and within an hour of being there, I was attacked by six boys from my school. This would be the final time it happened. This negative attitude towards me had to end and it did. I became stronger and determined to grow in myself. I became more out spoken, not shying away. I developed a cheeky attitude. The teachers and new people in my life where drawn to me. I joined the drama club and became part of productions the school put on for the local public. I started to find me. My positive attitude drew new people into my path and drew me closer to spirit (Little did I know). From a shy, scared little boy, I

Using Your Intuition By Psychic Medium Tony Hindley

In the Beginning

Became an outspoken, cheeky chap (As the teachers would call me). I had more friends than ever, friends who would protect me and be there and who certainly wouldn't let me run home from school feeling scared. These new people in my life knew something I didn't, they knew I was different and by different I mean Gay.

The reason I am expressing this to you, is because suddenly out of nowhere the lady I thought had vanished was in fact back with me. The reason I couldn't see her for a while, is simply because she had to step back, step back for me to learn life lessons and to understand my connection and experience. Once I became the cheeky, outspoken young man, she was there beside me, she had passed onto me her attitude in life and her character.

Using Your Intuition By Psychic Medium Tony Hindley

In the Beginning

"We may not be able to see spirit all the time, but in fact when we need them the most they are certainly still there, walking silently with us and guiding us" - Tony Hindley

There was one lady in my life and who I was lucky to have thirteen years with and that Lady is my Great Grandmother Mary Hindley. Out of all the people in my life, she was the one who knew who I was. I remember sitting beside her and she told me "Antony only ever be yourself, never try to be anything else, if you don't you'll be unhappy" Those words stick with me to this day and will never leave. Then sadly at the fantastic age of 97 my Great Grandmother had to leave her Physical body and leave her life behind with me and my family, her new purpose had to begin. I was thirteen and devastated she had to leave me behind, but she then gave me a new purpose, She became my spirit guide. At the age of thirteen I started to

Using Your Intuition By Psychic Medium Tony Hindley

In the Beginning

Give readings to my friends and to people I would meet during my work experience. I was handed my first ever set of Tarot Cards and this is where it all began.

Using Your Intuition By Psychic Medium Tony Hindley

The development begins

The rest of the book will focus on my own personal development, it will give you ideas on how to conduct in your own personal life. It will allow you to get an understanding on how I developed my connection and how I live my physical life along side my own spiritual connections. This is written in my own words and is how I see spirituality, this is not to dismiss what you believe in and your direction. This is a guide to my development and if I just help one person to understand, then I have achieved my purpose and my reasons for writing this book will be successful.

Over the years I have realised that three main things have helped me develop naturally, within my connection to the spirit world.

Gratitude *– Holding gratitude within, regarding my life path and spiritual path, has given me the inner positive connection. Be grateful for all the*

Using Your Intuition By Psychic Medium Tony Hindley

The development begins

Things you have in life, big or small. Working with gratitude has assisted my development. Giving out gratitude for my gift has opened many doors for me within this path. A simple thank you, out loud or within the mind, tells spirit you are truly grateful for their connections to you. You don't have to say thank you out loud, as telepathy can be heard. Be grateful for anything spirit gives to you! (This keeps you grounded)

Trust *– Try not to doubt yourself when working with spirit. If you doubt yourself, then you are in fact doubting, your guides, gate keepers and Spirit connections. I understand it's easy to doubt what is within your mind, is it your imagination or is it spirit. How I have dealt with this over the years is by, relaxing, opening my mind and telling spirit I am their vessel. Think of yourself as the employee to spirit, that you are*

Using Your Intuition By Psychic Medium Tony Hindley

The development begins

Working for the truest, highest and most honest beings.

Understanding – *I do not and will never understand what I do, I have given up on trying to understand why spirit have given me such a connection. I believe I am not meant to know. If I did I feel it would be taken away from me. Remember we can't and won't ever fully understand this connection. We don't control this, spirit do. Keeping this in your mind will ensure the Ego some mediums hold, won't over take you.*

Over the years I have met many people who claim to be Psychic or a Medium. In fact there are many different types of connections to the spirit world. Below is how I see the connections and how they have been explained to me, by my guides.

Using Your Intuition By Psychic Medium Tony Hindley

The development begins

Clairvoyance (Vision) – Having the ability to see spirit energies within the mind's eye, having the ability to see images, words or objects within the mind's eye. Having the ability to trust and read from these images.

Clairsentient (Feeling – Touch) – Having the ability to feel spirit energies around them, having the ability to feel atmosphere change, having the ability to feel the future changes within life. Giving the ability to read a person. By feeling the atmosphere around the person.

Clairaudience (Hearing – Listening) – Having the ability to hear spirit energies around them, having the ability to heighten the hearing to listen beyond our world.

Clairescence (Smell – Taste) – Having the ability to smell spirit energies around them, having the ability to smell / taste the change within the atmosphere.

Using Your Intuition By Psychic Medium Tony Hindley

The development begins

Psychic (Fortune) – I believe this to be, having the connection to all of the above and to hold the ability to read a persons, Past – Present and

Future. Having the ability to read from Tarot Cards, Angel Cards, Crystal balls etc.

Psychic Medium (All Knowing) – Having the ability to connect to all of the above and also holding the ability to speak directly to the spirit world, by using the many different ways of connection. Often communicating to their "Spirit Guides"

Using Your Intuition By Psychic Medium Tony Hindley

Spiritual Protection

As in our physical life, there are also negative connections to the spiritual world, not all spiritual connections are here to help they may wish to attach. So Spiritual protection is a must when connecting and developing your ability. Spiritual protection is in place by the spirit world to keep our soul and life path safe and connected, it is like your own personal body guard and you don't have to have plenty of money to have it, it's free.

It is very easy to call upon and it is something I advise you to do. Below is a quote that I use when calling upon my Spiritual protection.

"I call upon the connections to the spiritual life, I ask for my loved ones and guides to please step forward. I ask they you keep me safe and protected on my spiritual path and direction. I trust and believe in you"

Using Your Intuition By Psychic Medium Tony Hindley

Spiritual Protection

A little verse like that will give you the protection that your spiritual direction needs. All you need to do is BELIEVE in it and it will keep your Aura free from negative energies.

When I am saying this within my mind or out loud, I relax and close my eyes. I imagine all the positive souls connected to me, standing around me, facing me and linking an unbreakable circle around me.

Over the years what I imagine has changed. I once imagined myself standing in a dark room and that dark room filling with light as bright as bright can be, then I changed to me sitting in a green house and the plants growing and covering my physical body, this represented a protection from mother earth. Other things to imagine,

Using Your Intuition By Psychic Medium Tony Hindley

Spiritual Protection

- Being wrapped in cotton wool
- Angels standing before you
- Floating in water
- Bright light of colour shining from you
- Being hugged by loved ones or loved pets

There are many ways in which you can imagine your spiritual protection, it just has to be something that makes you feel safe, nice, warm and something or someone your trust.

Once you have found your connection to the Spiritual protection, you need to do this every time you connect to the spirit world. whether this be

- Self Development
- Conducting a reading
- Taking part in a Paranormal Event (Ghost Hunt)

This is so that every time you connect your spirit guides know you trust them and believe.

Using Your Intuition By Psychic Medium Tony Hindley

Spirit energies I work with

On this spiritual path, you will work alongside many different spiritual energies. Energies who allow us to connect with the spirit world and our loved ones who have walked the Earth. Here I have wrote a list of the energies I work alongside and how I see their connection to me (us).

Protectors – *I call upon the energy of my protectors on a daily basis and do this throughout the day. I believe that when I call upon them, they bring forward a much higher protection. A protection that can only be seen by the spirit world. This shows the spirit world that I am protected by a higher being, I work within the pure white light of the angels. Ensuring that negative or undesirable energies, understand my aura is not for their use.*

Using Your Intuition By Psychic Medium Tony Hindley

Spirit energies I work with

Gate Keepers – *I call upon my gate keepers to, keep the connection between myself and the spirit world calm. I ask them to close the gate between our world and theirs, when I am "closing" my connection down. When I "open" my connection, I ask them to step forward and open the gates. I feel if I didn't do this and if I didn't believe in my gate keepers, my connection would become very hectic, so in other words, they keep order.*

Guides – *When communicating with the spirit world. I believe and trust that I work alongside spirit energies known as "Guides" People often think we have one guide, but over the years I have realised I have multiple guides around me. Each one holding their own personal skill and gift. For example, when I do a reading, I call upon my guide of all knowing, she has the ability to take my connection on a journey, past,*

Using Your Intuition By Psychic Medium Tony Hindley

Spirit energies I work with

Present and future. Then when I do my Paranormal Investigations, I call upon her, but I also ask my guide who connects directly with the building I am investigating. Like my very own Inspector. So as you can see I work with many different "Guides". I feel these are the connections that make this possible for me.

Angels – *I believe that Angels are also our guides to life and our protectors. I believe that they are not male or female, they are how we see them or imagine them. When you hear the term "Life guide" I believe this is what the angels are doing for us, they guide us. When you feel that you need to change your life or change a situation you are in. I truly and deeply believe that our Angels are telling us we need to change path. This being the reason I use the term "Life Guide". When you're walking home at night and you feel you don't want to walk the normal*

Using Your Intuition By Psychic Medium Tony Hindley

Spirit energies I work with

Route and then the morning after you hear of something bad or negative happening on that route. This to me shows your Angels are protecting and guiding you through your path. Believe in your Angels, they work alongside you more than you realise.

Archangels – *There are many different levels to the Angels. The most common one known by man are the Archangels. When calling upon these, you don't have to use their name, like Michael, Raphael, etc. You can just ask for the Archangels to step forward and give assistance. They have many skills and abilities that will assist you through your life path. I also ask for Archangel Michaels help, when I am doing house clearances.*

I believe that the guides I work alongside are of a higher level, I believe they have many different abilities and many different way of communication. I trust and believe I am

Using Your Intuition By Psychic Medium Tony Hindley

Spirit energies I work with

Protected and I trust in the angels. The way I have been able to meet my guides and angels is through Meditation. I believe that any of the above can come forward as our loved ones.

Using Your Intuition By Psychic Medium Tony Hindley

Meditation

Over the years I have found that one main key to your own personal spiritual development is during meditation. During meditation wonderful things can happen. You can allow your mind to take you to places you have never been before. Yes meditation needs an open and relaxed mind, but trust me this is where the gift truly develops. My meditation goes back to when I was just a child, my mother would speak of how I am a "deep sleeper", yes back then this is what it would be seen as, but in fact I know now my mind was meditating when I was sleeping.

I can always remember something very significant about my past. I was thirteen years of age and I can remember this like it was yesterday. My Great-grandmother "Mary" had recently transitioned into spirit. I went to bed that evening, crying, emotional, heart aching, you name it I was feeling it. I quickly drifted off into my sleep. I was then greeted by my Great

Using Your Intuition By Psychic Medium Tony Hindley

Meditation

Grandmother. She was standing outside the local bank (Of all places). Smiling at me and waving, shouting "I'm fine honest". I remember waking with a sense of joy and happiness. Some people say this was a dream, but to this day I believe it was the start of my connections to meditation. Meditation doesn't only allow yourself development to grow, it cleanses you and dismisses negative energies and feelings. If this was a dream, I would of woken with the same heart ache I went to sleep with, but I didn't.

As a child I would only ever go to sleep with the TV or CD player on. Now I understand that back then my connections to meditation where with me. The vibrations of the music or sound, was allowing my mind to relax and drawing forward the meditation state of mind.

Using Your Intuition By Psychic Medium Tony Hindley

Meditation

These days my meditation will take place during the day or just before I sleep. Here is how you can go into meditation and allow your mind, body and soul to relax.

Firstly you need to set the setting, you can do this by the following ways

- Turn the lights down or off
- Light candles to set a sense of warmth about you (Not if you are going to sleep)
- Place incense in the room (white sage, sandalwood are good for this)
- Meditation music playing in the background (I use Tibetan singing bowl meditation)
- Sit on a comfy chair or lay down
- Both feet on the floor to allow your body to ground itself

Using Your Intuition By Psychic Medium Tony Hindley

Meditation

- Hands in your lap with palms facing up, this allows the energy to travel in the correct direction and shows spirit you accept the connection
- Close your eyes take three breaths and relax

This may come easy to some of you, but for some it may take you a few times to allow your body to relax. Once your meditation connection comes into direction, you will be able to meditate whenever and wherever you like. Make notes of the things you see, hear and feel. As it's always nice to look back on the meditation journey that is personal to you.

What I do need to say is that meditation can play with your emotions so please if you feel you are going too deep too quick, don't do meditation every day. Allow the energy to build and not be rushed.

Using Your Intuition By Psychic Medium Tony Hindley

Power Animal

Your power animal is connected to you and has been connected / assigned to you since your birth. They have grown with you and developed alongside you. Your power animal can step forward at anytime. They can step forward without you even calling on them. This is due to their unique ability to protect and guide.

Have you ever been drown to a certain animal?

Do you understand why are drawn to them?

Using Your Intuition By Psychic Medium Tony Hindley

Power Animal

If you have this is more than likely your Power animal showing themselves to you in physical form. Your Power animal can link to you on a level in which your guides and other spirit energies can't. They actually allow you to channel their own personalities and traits. For example: if your power animal is a Dog, it is showing that you are a very loyal person, you have a caring nature. You don't mind spending time with groups of people or on your own.

Using Your Intuition By Psychic Medium Tony Hindley

Power Animal

If your power animal is a Wolf, It is showing you like to be in control and you like to be a leader. You have the ability to control your life, but sometimes being too curious you can make the wrong decisions. But in the end the wolf has the strength and courage to continue and make that wrong a right.

Your power animal can be in the form of any animal, they can also be your beloved pets that have transitioned into the spirit world. Some people tell me that they have many power animals, this can happen. It happens when your undergoing changes within your own personal life. The reason they can change is simply because each animal has its own traits and depending what your life is bringing forward, will change the traits you need within your path at that time.

So on that note let's try to link and find your power animal that is with you at this moment.

Using Your Intuition By Psychic Medium Tony Hindley

Power Animal

We all connect to our power animals in different ways, but here is the way I connect, this could assist you.

Firstly, I will sit and relax my mind, body and soul. Following the directions given early regarding meditation. Before you conduct meditation, within your mind or out loud say

"I ask my guides to draw forward and show my power animal connection during my meditation"

Using Your Intuition By Psychic Medium Tony Hindley

Power Animal

This is your way of wanting your power animal to stand by you, this also shows your guides you Are wanting them to help and assist with this connection. Remember your guides want to work with you and will assist you like you assist them.

Remember to write information down in a little pad so you can look back on your spiritual journey.

Using Your Intuition By Psychic Medium Tony Hindley

Working alongside Spirit Guides

To this very day I can remember the day I met my first guide. I say my first guide, as just like our school years we change teachers and have different teachers for different subjects. So as you develop and you grow within your spiritual path, you will change guides who will connect you to different ways of connecting with the spirit world.

My first guide who I met and who is still with me is "Athena" very strong and visits me often. She appears to me in a light green dress with green flames, she is pale skinned, brown long flowing hair and ice blue eyes, a medium build to her structure and she is 5ft 9.

I call on Athena to assist me when I conduct my readings, when I feel I need a spiritual protection and when I am working during the evening. you may read this and think to yourself, this sounds strange, but as strange as

Using Your Intuition By Psychic Medium Tony Hindley

Working alongside Spirit Guides

It may sound, I know this is her as I believe in her and the spirit world about me.

People may say to you that we only have one guide, I am not telling you this is wrong, I am simply saying in my experience we have many who will help and assist in different directions.

Meditation allowed me to connect with my guides so much easier, as they stepped forward during this time and I made notes in my little book to remember the details I had been given.

Have you ever had a feeling of someone watching you, but you felt safe and secure? This is more than likely your guide saying to you "I'm here". They will step in during your darkest days in life, during positive situations, in fact they will step in whenever you want them to. All you need to do is Believe.

Using Your Intuition By Psychic Medium Tony Hindley

Working alongside Spirit Guides

Our guides can work alongside us within our own personal life and also within our spiritual direction. They can assist in many different ways, from linking you with someone's past, present, future all the way to giving you courage and confidence within a job. How this works we will never fully understand but all you need to do is believe they will and have been helping you since your birth.

Over a period of time we grow from a baby to an adult and during that process we allow our minds to be told, "that isn't true" "It's not real" so we become ignorant towards what is about us and close down from the spirit world. I was lucky as my family never told me what I saw wasn't real, they just agreed and allowed my development to take place.

So by reading this book it is showing that your mind is open to the spirit world and that is a

Using Your Intuition By Psychic Medium Tony Hindley

Working alongside Spirit Guides

Positive start in your development and direction. We can do many things to allow our guides to step in and connect with us. There are a few things that I do but this may not work for everyone, but you can find your own way and mine is just a guideline. Like the title of this book you "Use your intuition"

In chapter one we spoke about mediation and its positive direction, this is the first thing I suggest to connect to your guides. This will allow them to show themselves to you and allows your mind to accept them. It's much easier for spirit to step in if you are relaxed and calm. This over time will be much easier as your development connects. Once you have your room set and ready for your meditation, you can say a few words before hand, these words will let the spirit world know you are ready to connect. things like,

Using Your Intuition By Psychic Medium Tony Hindley

Working alongside Spirit Guides

"I ask my guides to step forward during my meditation, allow me to hear, see and feel your connection"

I"I believe and trust within your connection"

"Allow my mind, body and soul to open to you my guide"

"I trust myself and I trust you"

This shows spirit about you that you are willing to connect, it shows your guides that you will accept the time it takes for them to connect with you. We have to remember that this could be new to them as well and not only new to you. Time has no limit in the spirit world, so allow them to work at their own pace.

The key to your development is "Do not rush or expect too much"

Using Your Intuition By Psychic Medium Tony Hindley

Working alongside Spirit Guides

There are several other ways in which I assisted my development and connection to my spirit guides. I would read over and over the details they had given me through meditation, I would talk about this to others (even if they thought I

was going mad). I would sit in class and within my mind I would say things like,

"Athena are you with me now"

"Athena I believe your standing beside me"

"Athena show me a butterfly"

All the time I didn't know it but my guides where listening to me and they were showing me signs all around. One day I had asked for a sign she was with me, I ask for her to show me a bright coloured butterfly. It was during my Art GCSE exam, I was sat scribbling away designing my piece. I turned around and the girl behind me had drawn (Perfectly may I add) a butterfly,

Using Your Intuition By Psychic Medium Tony Hindley

Working alongside Spirit Guides

Bright in colour, emerging from bright green flames. Some people see this as a coincidence, but I believe this was Athena assisting the drawing and showing herself by placing the thought of green flames and a bright butterfly just as I asked.

So as you can see I was asking for a butterfly but Athena my guide brought this forward to me in a very different way. What this means is if you ask your guides to show they are around you, be open and be vigilant as it will and can come

forward in strange ways. Please give time for it to come forward to you, as again time in spirit has no limit, so to us it may take days, but to them it's only been a few minutes.

Another way which may work for you is, leaving little notes to them. Find an object that you are drawn to, whether it be a small statue, a little clock or even a jewellery box. Write down

Using Your Intuition By Psychic Medium Tony Hindley

Working alongside Spirit Guides

On a piece of paper "I ask for my guide to draw forward to me" then fold this and place it under the object. Then within your mind just say, "I have left you my guide a small note under the (State the object" Leave this note as long as you like, sometimes you may even forget about it,

but this isn't a bad thing. Spirit will then use intuition to read your note.

Again this shows your guides you are willing for them to step forward it also shows you believe in them. The more you show willing the more they will realise you are ready for your connection. We all have a spiritual connection, it just takes time for us to open that channel.

Using Your Intuition By Psychic Medium Tony Hindley

Meditation / Healing Room

Meditation rooms / Healing rooms are something I have always worked in and use to meditate, These rooms a sacred to you. Over time the room will generate the energy that is needed for your own personal development. You don't need to have a room like this for self development, it is just something I do as I like to have a little lay down when meditating.

So within the picture you will notice certain things I have in the room, here I will explain why I have them.

Buddha Picture - I believe that Arch Angel Buddha helps your development and connects you to the spiritual side you have within you. So

By having this in the room, it shows Buddha I am willing to accept his blessings and spiritual connections.

Candles - I use candles a lot and this allows the negative energies around us to be dismissed.

Using Your Intuition By Psychic Medium Tony Hindley

Meditation / Healing Room

Candles also draw forward a spiritual protection that creates a wall between our physical body and our spirit path.

CD Player - I use this to play relaxing music within the background. This is to allow my mind to focus and draw forward my meditation state of mind. This relaxing doesn't only allow your body to relax, it also allows your soul to be lifted and drawn closer to your spirit guides during your development.

Incense - I burn incense during my meditation, this again brings a relaxing state of mind but will also cleanse your aura. I normally use "white sage" or "Sandalwood. I use these as they smell

Nice and they also have natural healing / cleansing properties.

Using Your Intuition By Psychic Medium Tony Hindley

Meditation / Healing Room

Healing Bed - This is simply for comfort and relaxation. You don't need to have a healing bed, a chair will be suitable.

Plant / Water - I have these in the room as they naturally purify the room, they cleanse the room and draw forward the spirit energies. Water is a very good connection to the spirit world and spirit tend to draw forward to the natural connection the plant / water has to mother earth.

Crystals - I have two different crystals in my room, "Clear Quartz" the crystal of all knowing and spiritual protection. "Amethyst" the crystal

of spiritual connection. This crystal when close by will automatically draw forward your spiritual connection and also draws a natural spiritual protection.

Using Your Intuition By Psychic Medium Tony Hindley

Meditation / Healing Room

In the image above, you will see how my meditation / healing rooms is set out. Look closely at the things I have in the room.

Using Your Intuition By Psychic Medium Tony Hindley

Development

There are many ways you can develop your spiritual connection. Whether it be through development circles, self development through meditation, strengthening techniques. All will assist you and direct you into your path. But you need to ensure you remain grounded and connected to your roots. Don't become a clone of someone else. Your connection to spirit is unique to you and not one connection is the same as each other.

A lot of people may tell you are doing it wrong or you should do it this way. This is incorrect as what works for one person, may not work for someone else. You may think this book is doing just that, but it isn't. This book is to show you ways in which I have developed my connection and to give you ideas on how you can strengthen yours. The title of the book is "Using your intuition" so by reading this book you will

Using Your Intuition By Psychic Medium Tony Hindley

Development

Be drawn to ways in which you feel could work for you and the ways that don't just mean it isn't for you. But by trusting your gut instinct and following your intuition you will see and feel the correct ways.

Growing up I never visited Spiritual Circles or had any Spiritual Friends. My guides developed me and connected me to them, they allowed me to develop in a natural way. As I grew older I became more understanding of what was happening around me. I visited certain spiritual centres and met new people, each person giving me ideas on how to strengthen my connection.

Using Your Intuition By Psychic Medium Tony Hindley

Development

Candle Technique

Firstly you need a candle to conduct this.

- *Place the candle on a hard level surface*
- *Light the candle and turn the lights off*
- *Sit facing the candle*
- *You can have incenses burn and meditation music if you wish*
- *Take three deep breaths though the nose and exhale through the mouth .*

Then as you focus on the centre of the candle flame, looking directly at the wick. Imagine the flame burning any negative energies and feelings from within. Clearing your mind and clearing your Aura of negative energies. As you breathe in and out, imagine the flame entering your inner body and burning and cleansing your soul. This will allow the energies to flow much easier.

Using Your Intuition By Psychic Medium Tony Hindley

Development

Candle Technique

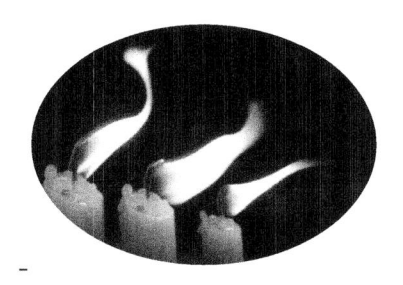

Focusing on the candle for 3 to 5 minutes. You then relax and close your eyes. Within the distant you will see the flame burning. As the flame begins to fade, ask within your mind

"Bring the flame back, allow it to burn within my mind and mind's eye"

By doing this it will bring focus and strengthen something called "The mind's eye" This I will explain in a moment.

As the flame vanishes from sight, reopen your eyes and focus again, repeating the technique. Doing this over and over again will strengthen

Using Your Intuition By Psychic Medium Tony Hindley

Development

"Mind's Eye"

The "Mind's Eye" Over a period of time you may feel a slight throbbing in the centre of your forehead or even a slight headache. This is normal when doing this technique.

The Mind's eye is also known as the "Third Eye". This is directly between your eyes but deep under the skin. You may often hear a Medium or Psychic use the term "I am seeing this within my mind's eye". This simply means that they are seeing an image or a scene being acted out within the mind. Your mind's eye can see things your actual eyes can't see.

So how I have come to understood this is. Imagine you are out with friends and you are seeing the scenes around you and taking everything in through your eyes, Then all of a sudden you start seeing a different scene around you but you know that you aren't within

Using Your Intuition By Psychic Medium Tony Hindley

Development

"Mind's Eye"

That scene. This is your mind's eye showing you something that was once there or is going to be there, It is like you have your own cinema screen behind your eyes but in front of the brain. As

You use the candle technique it will strengthen the "Mind's Eye". This is why you may feel a throbbing or a slight headache between the eye's, as this is a sign that the Mind's Eye is opening and connecting to the spirit world around you. Once you have this connection spirit will step in much closer to you and you will find the connection much easier and stronger. Again this may not work for everyone, but it is a guide in your direction.

Using Your Intuition By Psychic Medium Tony Hindley

Development

"Mind's Eye"

Below in the image I have pointed out where the Third Eye / Mind's Eye is situated. Over time as we grow we lose connection to this space, so by channelling the connection it will start to "Reopen". Don't worry it won't be an actual eye upon your face, it is hidden.

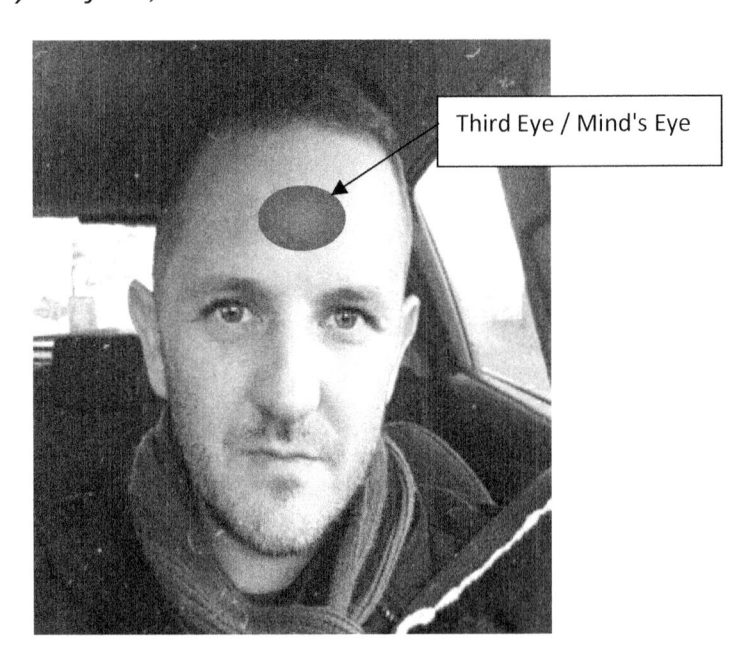

Third Eye / Mind's Eye

Using Your Intuition By Psychic Medium Tony Hindley

Development

As you continue with your development you will experience many different things, that will be unique to you and not be the same to others about you. Your body may also go through many changes and your personality may change. This is natural as your body adjust and your spiritual connections open.

"Aura Technique"

The Aura is an energy field that is around anything living, even though objects such as, Plant pots, keys, rings, these will have an energy field due to us as beings holding and using these objects. The Aura has many layers, this technique will strengthen the connection to the Aura and assist your "mind's eye" development.

" An aura or Human energy field is, according to New Age beliefs, a coloured emanation said to enclose a human body or any animal or object." - Quoted from Google

Using Your Intuition By Psychic Medium Tony Hindley

Development

"Aura Technique"

- *Place the candle on a hard level surface*
- *Light the candle and turn the lights off*
- *Sit facing the candle*
- *You can have incenses burn and meditation music if you wish*
- *Take three deep breaths though the nose and exhale through the mouth .*
- *Focus on the flame of the candle looking into the wick*
- *Do this for 3 to 5 minutes*
- *Hold your hand up in front of you focusing on the tips of your fingers*
- *Keep flicking your eyes away from your hand and then back*
- *A wave will gradually appear (The energy) leaving the fingers*
- *Over time colours should or will start to appear*

Using Your Intuition By Psychic Medium Tony Hindley

Development

"Aura Technique"

Doing this over a period of time will again connect your vision to your Mind's Eye. This technique does take some time to develop, so my advice to you is to persevere and remember, it takes time and don't rush your connection.

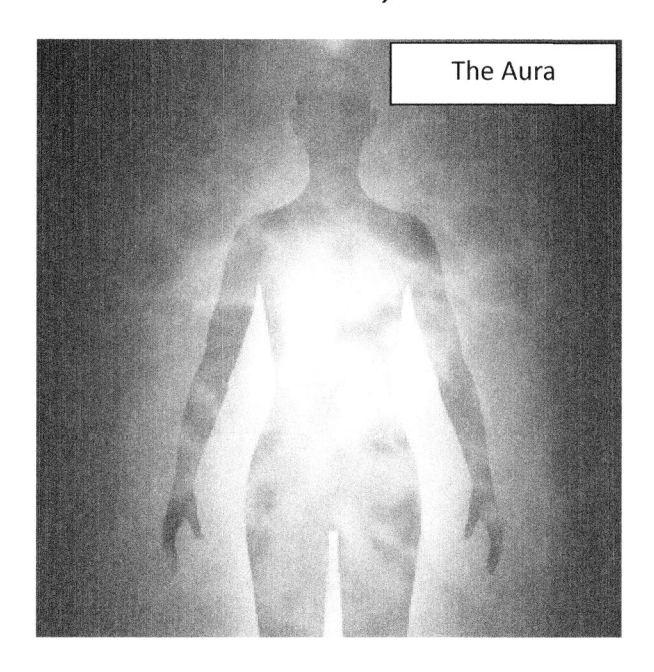

The Aura

Using Your Intuition By Psychic Medium Tony Hindley

Development

"Aura Technique"

The way in which I can describe is, when there is a very hot day and your walking along, you can see the heat rising from the ground. This creates a wave within the atmosphere. This is how Aura's appear to me, I see this wave around a person's body and sometimes comes with bright colours.

Using Your Intuition By Psychic Medium Tony Hindley

Development

"Intuition"

When linking to the spirit world and connecting in your own way, one thing that is always the same with us all is, trusting your gut and intuition. The gut plays a big part when making decisions in your life path and also plays a big part in your spiritual direction. I have walked through life telling others around me that the head rules the heart and the heart rules the head. So I always express trust your gut regarding changes, thoughts, feelings and more. Walking through life we don't realise we use the gut in everyday life and we sometimes ignore the instinct, here is a technique I use for strengthening the gut and intuition.

Using Your Intuition By Psychic Medium Tony Hindley

Development

"Intuition"

"Intuition & Gut Instinct Technique"

- *Sit in a room with candle/s lit*
- *Burn incense and have relaxing music in the background*
- *Take three deep breaths in through the nose and exhale through the mouth*
- *Allow your body to relax and your mind clear*
- *Then in your mind ask a question, Example "Are my guides standing with me"?*
- *Trust the first answer you get*
- *Then change the answer, So if the answer is "Yes" in your mind start saying "No" over and over again*
- *This is where the gut will kick in, you will feel a feeling in your stomach telling you that you are not listening and trying to change the reply*
- *Then repeat the answer given over and over in your mind and the feeling will subside.*

Using Your Intuition By Psychic Medium Tony Hindley

Development

"Intuition"

What I will advise is, don't ask personal questions till you are 100% connected to your gut instinct and intuition, as you can manipulate the answer given without even realising. You can change the answer if you are very passionate about something that is occurring within your life and allow you heart and head to rule.

Continue the technique given and you will develop a link to your intuition, a link you will find interesting once fully connected.

Using Your Intuition By Psychic Medium Tony Hindley

Angel / Guide Altar

During my development I have come to understand many different ways of showing acceptance and respect to your guides and angels about you. Showing this shows that you are willing for them to work alongside you. Whether this be within connection or by everyday life. You have to remember they like to be involved in your life and will assist you as much as they can.

Believe it or not your guides and angels have been working alongside you before you came into this physical world. They have been assigned to you, just like a teacher is assigned his/her class. As you grow your Spirit energies grow with you and develop their own personal connections as well. But as you need to move onto a new stage in your development, your guides and angels may shift. Just like being at school, you move class and you move teachers, but the teachers who have been in your life will

Using Your Intuition By Psychic Medium Tony Hindley

Angel / Guide Altar

Remain there and never leave during your development.

During my time developing with my gift, many people spoke to me about Angel Altars. This is a place you can communicate with your Angels and Guides, where you can ask for assistance or just to connect with them. I have made a list of things you need to create your very own Angel Altar and below is an image of mine.

Using Your Intuition By Psychic Medium Tony Hindley

Angel / Guide Altar

Angel Altar – Angel Altars are a place in which you can ask your Angels / Guides for assistance and shows them you are grateful of their personal connection to you. The main things to have to build your own Angel Altar:

- Candle/s
- Incense and holder
- Statue of an Angel
- Crystal
- A desk or side table to place your Altar on
- Anything else you are drawn to and wish to be on your Altar

You then relax with your eyes closed and ask the Angels / Guides within your mind. "How would you like me to arrange your Altar? Open your eyes and you will feel where everything needs to be placed. Within minutes your Altar will be completed. You can now start to communicate with them. Sitting with your Altar, lighting the

Using Your Intuition By Psychic Medium Tony Hindley

Angel / Guide Altar

Candles and incenses. Will show the Angels / Guides you are needing them or wanting to communicate. You can even write a question / ask for their help on paper and place the paper under the statue for the angels to read. Don't remove the paper before your question is answered / help is given. If you ever feel something needs to come off or something needs to be added, do it, as it's you're Angels telling you and not your feeling! Remember Trust!

Using Your Intuition By Psychic Medium Tony Hindley

How I see Your Higher self

Your higher self is you. Your higher self is the real you, your total soul. The physical you that is living here on Earth is just a projection of your higher self. Your higher self is more complete than you can imagine, the one that isn't being frustrated by the events in our physical life. The higher self is the one in charge of your spiritual contract and the life you planned before your physical self. They are the ones that hold onto your life plan and your spiritual direction and path.

Your Higher Self is not male or female, but I find it much easier to refer to my higher self as my current gender "Male".

Why we live our physical life, our higher self is within a much high level, they are within the vibrations of the spiritual connection, where we was, before we were assigned our life.

Using Your Intuition By Psychic Medium Tony Hindley

How I see Your Higher self

There is and will always be an unbreakable bond between yourself and your higher self. This is because the higher self is your higher connection to the higher levels, levels in which we don't fully understand and probably won't ever understand fully.

Your higher self is the one that keeps you on your path, the path you planned with them before your physical body here on earth. Whether you believe in fate or feel you have seen something before, this is because you have already lived this path. You lived the path when you planned it. The people we meet, the things we gain, our goals, the lessons we learn. These have all been planned before you were born into this world we know as Earth.

The connection between you and your higher self?

Yourself and your higher self is connected by the link between your spiritual soul. As we see

Using Your Intuition By Psychic Medium Tony Hindley

How I see Your Higher self

Ourselves in our physical body, you have to look much deeper to see your soul. The soul that lives within is only a percentage of the true you. A percentage that has been assigned this role on earth. The rest of the percentage is the higher you, which is looking down on you and watching you as you learn lessons, develop bonds, achieve the goals in the life. Even when you feel you have "Done the wrong thing" "Taken the wrong direction". Your higher self is ensuring you are placed back on the path you set yourself. The only connection we have with our higher self is a connection through the spiritual levels. As we are born we don't remember this connection, but through life you will feel like "you have been here before" or seen something happen before it does. Many of us brush this off, but I see this as your Higher self calling and trying to reconnect to you.

Using Your Intuition By Psychic Medium Tony Hindley

How I see Your Higher self

How I connect to my Higher Self

Again a lot of my connections are via meditation and then once this connection is stronger it becomes more natural.

Remember your Higher self is on a spiritual level so by meditating it will allow your higher self to come to your level. Allowing your body, mind and soul to relax, make yourself comfortable. Close your eyes and start to visualise simple things like,

- *A table and chairs where you can sit*
- *A bench in a park or dark room*
- *A room you are familiar with*

This is so you can call on your higher self to come and sit with you in comfort.

At first you may find this difficult and strange, but please continue as once you have this connection, you have the link to you and your life plan that you set yourself before your connection to earth.

I will be honest this took me a while to understand and it took me a while to link to the

Using Your Intuition By Psychic Medium Tony Hindley

How I see Your Higher self

Higher self. So don't worry and don't feel you're doing anything wrong.
The main thing you need to do is "Listen" you will hear a voice coming from within, this may sound like you or sound like someone you know. Your Higher self will speak in a voice you understand and don't fear. At first you will think and feel this is your own imagination talking to you. The way you can understand what is your higher self, is by using your intuition and gut instinct, connect to them feelings. Over time you will feel that this is your higher self. To date when I connect with my higher self I feel a breeze around me and my body reacts by giving me goose bumps.
You will see a connection that is unique to you.

Over time you will ask questions to your higher self and you will feel the advice given is from the higher you. Your ego and doubt will subside. The advice will sound very knowledgeable, more than you usually sound.

Using Your Intuition By Psychic Medium Tony Hindley

How I see Your Higher self

This will take time and practice so keep going and all will connect at the right time, in the right place.

How will your higher self show his or herself ?

Your higher self will show themselves to you however you imagine them. My first encounter with myself they stepped forward looking like my Great Grandmother, someone I knew and someone I feel and felt safe around. Now my higher self appears to me as a voice coming from within and during meditation I see energy blending together.
How you see your higher self is unique to you and won't be the same as anyone else. This is your higher self and your soul energy.

Is my higher self forever with me?

Trust me when I say to you, your higher self will always remain with you. whether you choose to connect to them or not. They are part of your

Using Your Intuition By Psychic Medium Tony Hindley

How I see Your Higher self

Soul being and they are a percentage of your connection to this path. Trust and believe in yourself and trust and believe in your connection.

Take time out for yourself and your Higher self

As we do with our guides and loved ones, you need to take some time out for yourself and your higher self. This is to ensure your connection is there and to ensure your spiritual development. Your higher self may decide to "Bob in" from time to time without warning. ways in which they have done this to me is

- *Before I sleep I will hear answers to my question I may of asked during the day.*

- *During my sleep they may come and visit during my dreams and give answers and directions.*

- *During my meditation*

Using Your Intuition By Psychic Medium Tony Hindley

How I see Your Higher self

- *When I connect with spirit and start my readings, they often jump into my mind before I start conducting the connection.*

Just imagine how life can connect once you have connected to your higher self. Remember keep going and all will fall into place, but remember we won't and can't fully understand.

Using Your Intuition By Psychic Medium Tony Hindley

Conclusion

During the course of reading this book, You will have been given the knowledge and information connected to my development. This may not work for everyone, but I have written this as a direction and not fact. I truly believe we are all unique in our paths and spiritual direction. I believe that we all develop in our own ways and development comes from all different directions.

What works for one person may not work for someone else. My main aim in writing this book was to show you that you must trust your own gut instinct and by doing that you will find your direction. Using your intuition is the key to help your personal development. Remain grounded and true at all times.

Each chapter has been written by myself to show you examples of what I do and how I connect to our loved ones, spirit energies and work alongside them.

Using Your Intuition By Psychic Medium Tony Hindley

Conclusion

The techniques I have shown you within this book are something that a lot of spiritual people use. Some find them easy and some find them difficult. But as in your own personal life don't give up, keep pushing and keep moving forward. Each time you sit to conduct one of the techniques spirit will see your willingness and they will one day step forward and truly show you the beauty of the spiritual path.

Remember your spiritual path isn't a path to be on alone, there are many people out there taking this journey with you. Each journey unique, each person you cross within your path has been placed there for a reason, whether they be in your life a long period of time or just a short time. Each one of them will bring forward a connection that has been needed for you. I once visited many Spiritual Development Circles and the collection of spiritual energy is a lovely feeling. This is where development grows also,

Using Your Intuition By Psychic Medium Tony Hindley

Conclusion

Everyone wanting the same thing and everyone wanting to connect to the spirit world. This is a strong energy and something I advise others to do. Remember use your instinct to direct you to the correct circle for you. As I always say not everyone's energy is compatible.

This is one reason I began running my own Spiritual Development Circle. I believe we are all on our own journey, but this unique journey joins people together on a much bigger journey.

"Trust yourself, Believe in yourself, remain strong and most of all, never give up"

Tony Hindley

"It's OK that thoughts don't manifest into reality immediately (if we saw a picture of an elephant and it instantly appeared, that would be too soon)" *- Quote from the book The Secret*

Using Your Intuition By Psychic Medium Tony Hindley

Connect With Tony Hindley

Facebook

Psychic Medium Tony Hindley

Supernatural Dairies Ghost Hunting Events

Website - For all information and events

www.supernaturaldiarie.wixsite.com/supernaturaldiaries

Email

supernaturaldiaries2014@yahoo.com

mediumtonyhindley@yahoo.co.uk

YouTube Us

Supernatural Diaries with Tony Hindley

Using Your Intuition By Psychic Medium Tony Hindley

Supernatural Diaries Team

As well as working as a Psychic Medium, I also work alongside my Paranormal Team. We conduct Ghost Hunting Events all over the UK.

In 2014 I decided to put together this team, I did this as I had been on may events with other companies and really enjoyed the evenings.

We do this to allow others to enjoy the work we do, we believe in working with a genuine connection and genuine purpose and our purpose is to bring people together not only in our physical life but also in our spirit life.

Each team member has their own personal connection and personal spiritual journey we are going on and together we enjoy having others join that journey with us. If you are interested in joining our journey please visit our website for all up and coming events.

We look forward to meeting you

Using Your Intuition By Psychic Medium Tony Hindley

The Supernatural Diaries Team

Left to Right

Dawn, Tony Hindley, Alison, Ryan

Michelle & Kevin

Using Your Intuition By Psychic Medium Tony Hindley

Photos

"Brian the Haunted Bear & Alfie

Our Guest at , Leigh Spinners Paranormal Night

Using Your Intuition By Psychic Medium Tony Hindley

Photos

Guest and Team, At 30 East Drive Paranormal Night

Energy Shift During Barlow Institute Paranormal Night

Using Your Intuition By Psychic Medium Tony Hindley

Photos

Guest during Tony's Audience with

Psychic Medium Tony Hindley

Tony's Usui Reiki Level II Students

Using Your Intuition By Psychic Medium Tony Hindley

Reference's

Page 5 - Quote from Albert Einstein / Google

Page's 32 - 35 - Tony's personal photos

Page 47 - Tony's personal photo

Page 51 - Google Image photo

Page 54 - Tony's personal photo

Page 57 - Google Image photo

Page 63 - Tony's personal photo

Page 75 - Tony's personal photo

Page 74 - Quote from the book "The Secret" Rhonda Byrne

Page's 78-81 - Tony's personal photos

Using Your Intuition By Psychic Medium Tony Hindley

Printed in Great Britain
by Amazon